CONTENTS

Some words are shown in bold, **like this**. You can find out what they mean by looking in the glossary.

WAR BREAKS OUT

On 1 September 1939, German armies invaded Poland. World War II had begun. In this war women fought, worked, suffered, and died alongside men. Millions of women faced dangers and challenges with courage.

By 1940, German armies had conquered most of Europe, and in 1941 attacked the Soviet Union. In December 1941, Japan attacked the US naval base at Pearl Harbor in Hawaii, and the United States joined the war. The global war made millions of women **refugees**. Many more faced hardship and danger in **occupied countries**.

Women go to war

The **Allied nations** summoned all their peoples to fight the war. Millions of men left home to join the army, navy, and air forces. Thousands of women also went into uniform. Millions of other women took over jobs that had usually been done by men – in the fire service, in **civil defence**, in factories and shipyards, in transport, and on farms. Many young women left home for the first time.

▲ Bus and rail stations were the scenes of many partings. The war meant years of separation. Many men were killed, and many wives became war **widows**.

Eyewitness

Most people heard the news of war in 1939 on the radio. A seventeen-year-old student-teacher in Essex, England, listened in the staff room at her school. News of the German bombing attacks on Poland reached the children. When she asked a class of thirteen to fourteen year-olds why they were not as well behaved as usual, one girl answered, "well, miss, you see, we might not be here next week."

Adapted from a diary entry, 1 September 1939.

1 September 1939
Germany invades Poland. Britain and France tell Germany to halt or face war. No reply comes from Germany.

3 September 1939
Britain and France declare war on Germany. At 11.15 a.m. in Britain, many women are cooking Sunday lunch. Air raid **sirens** sound, but it is a false alarm.

3 September 1939
Australia and New Zealand join the war on Britain's side, followed on 10 September by Canada.

THE WORLD AT WAR
WORLD WAR II

Women at War

.... Brenda Williams

www.heinemann.co.uk/library
Visit our website to find out more information about **Heinemann Library** books.

To order:
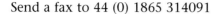 Phone 44 (0) 1865 888066
Send a fax to 44 (0) 1865 314091
Visit the Heinemann Bookshop at www.heinemann.co.uk/library to browse our catalogue and order online.

First published in Great Britain by Heinemann Library, Halley Court, Jordan Hill, Oxford OX2 8EJ, part of Harcourt Education.
Heinemann is a registered trademark of Harcourt Education Ltd.

Editorial: Andrew Farrow and Dan Nunn
Design: Lucy Owen and Tokay Interactive Ltd (www.tokay.co.uk)
Picture Research: Hannah Taylor and Sally Claxton
Production: Victoria Fitzgerald

Originated by Repro Multi Warna
Printed and bound in China by WKT Company Limited

The paper used to print this book comes from sustainable resources.

ISBN-13: 978 0 431 10375 4 (HB)
ISBN-10:   0 431 10375 5 (HB)
10 09 08 07 06
10 9 8 7 6 5 4 3 2 1

ISBN-13: 978 0 431 10382 2 (PB)
ISBN-10:   0 431 10382 8 (PB)
10 09 08 07
10 9 8 7 6 5 4 3 2 1

British Library Cataloguing in Publication Data
Williams, Brenda, 1946–
    Women at war. – (World at war. World War II)
    1. World War, 1939–1945 – Women – Juvenile literature 2. Women and war – Juvenile literature
    I. Title
    940.5'3'082
A full catalogue record for this book is available from the British Library.

Acknowledgements
The publishers would like to thank the following for permission to reproduce photographs:

Australian War Memorial p. **22**; Corbis pp. **4, 5** (Hulton Deutsch Collection), **7 bottom** (Condé Nast Archive), **16, 18 bottom, 19 top** (Hulton Deutsch Collection), **25 top** (Hulton Deutsch Collection), **28** (Hulton Deutsch Collection); Getty Images pp. **9** (Hulton Archive), **10 top** (Hulton Archive), **17** (Hulton Archive), **24** (Hulton Archive), **27 top** (Hulton Archive); Imperial War Museum pp. **10 bottom, 11 top, 21**; Mary Evans Picture Library p. **13**; National Army Museum p. **23 bottom**; Popperfoto pp. **6, 12, 14, 15 left**; Redferns Music Picture Library p. **25 bottom**; Source unknown p. **15 right**; The Art Archive pp. **19 bottom** (NARA), **27 bottom**; Topfoto.co.uk pp. **7 top** (Public Record Office/HIP), **11 bottom** (Public Record Office/HIP), **18 top** (Public Record Office/HIP), **26** (The Lord Price Collection); Topham Picturepoint pp. **8, 20, 23 top**.

Cover photograph of Wrens fitting smoke floats to a trainer aircraft at a Fleet Air Arm station, 1942, reproduced with permission of Popperfoto.

Every effort has been made to contact copyright holders of any material reproduced in this book. Any omissions will be rectified in subsequent printings if notice is given to the publishers.

Eyewitness

"I was standing on the carpet when the Pearl Harbor announcement was made ... I can remember looking at the carpet, and thinking my life would never be the same again."

American teenager Nancy Potter

▲ As German armies swept through Europe, women and children became refugees. Thousands took to the roads in whatever vehicles they could find, seeking safety from the fighting.

Waiting and wondering

Many married women were left to bring up families while men were away in the armed forces. Wives and mothers dreaded the **telegram**, letter, or phone call with news that a husband or son serving in the forces was dead or missing. Many men did not return from the war.

Although only women in the Soviet Union actually fought in battles, many other women showed tremendous courage. In many countries, women worked, shopped, and cooked as usual while at night bombs fell around their homes. World War II brought mass bombing from the air for the first time, and a bomb falling on a street killed women alongside men. Even when there were no bombs, women had to cope with shortages, **rationing**, learning new skills, and running a home alone. The "Home Front" was their battleground.

5

September 1939	April–June 1940	7 December 1941
Thousands of British women and children are evacuated from cities to the countryside.	German armies overrun Norway, Denmark, Holland, Belgium, and France. More than 300,000 Allied soldiers are rescued from Dunkirk in France.	The US Navy base at Pearl Harbor, Hawaii, is attacked by the Japanese. Next day, the United States declares war.

Making do

In many European countries there was soon a shortage of food, fuel, and many everyday items, such as stockings and soap. Factories switched from peacetime production to making guns, planes, tanks, and uniforms. With much less on offer in the shops, women managed with what they could buy, mend, or make themselves.

Rationing of food and clothing was enforced by law. In 1942, a British woman's food ration for a week included just 55 grams (2 ounces) of tea (roughly 15 teabags), 55 grams (2 ounces) (one portion) of cheese and one egg. In Britain, people were asked to bathe in just 12.5 centimetres (5 inches) of water – to save water. Silk stockings became so scarce that some women painted their bare legs with "liquid silk" dye.

Governments gave tips on how to make clothes from scraps of material and even blankets. Women knitted socks and scarves, patched old clothes, and stitched worn sheets.

▼ Hopeful shoppers gathered outside any shop that had something to sell. Most people accepted rationing as necessary, but complained about anyone who cheated.

▶ A wartime advertising slogan aimed at women was "Make-do and mend". A character called "Mrs Sew-and-Sew" was pictured in advertising campaigns. She showed women in Britain "How to patch Elbows and Trousers" or "How to Patch a Shirt". Shirts were easy, said Mrs Sew-and-Sew, because you could cut off a bit that didn't show to patch a hole.

MAKE-DO AND MEND

says Mrs. Sew-and-Sew

ISSUED BY THE BOARD OF TRADE

In the News

Advertising slogans aimed at women included:

- "Home Front hands can still be charming."
- "If you can knit, you can do your bit."
- "Grow fit not fat on your war diet!"

◀ Schoolgirls and women in America and Canada collected used clothes to make "Bundles for Britain", and knitted warm socks and scarves for servicemen. New clothes were rare because of bomb damage in Europe and because many factories had switched to making army uniforms, belts, kitbags, and other war material.

DANGER FROM THE AIR

World War II was the first war in which mass air attacks were made on cities. In these attacks, women were on the front line.

Britain's Blitz

In Britain, the raids during the **Blitz** of 1940–1941 were a frightening time for millions of people. German bombers often attacked by night, when streets were darkened in the **blackout**. This meant that many families went without proper sleep. Women living through the noise and shock of an air raid tried to keep calm, to comfort frightened children, and to act normally. It was a great strain, and an experience few ever forgot.

Courage at Pearl Harbor

Though US cities prepared for air raids, Japan and Germany had no bombers able to reach the United States. However, women at military bases in war zones were often in danger. For example, 82 US Army nurses were on duty when Japanese planes launched from aircraft carriers bombed Pearl Harbor in 1941. First Lieutenant Annie Fox, Chief Nurse at Hickam Field base, helped treat hundreds of injured men. For her "fine example of calmness, courage, and leadership" she was awarded the Purple Heart, a medal given only for outstanding behaviour in wartime. She was the first of many US Army nurses to be honoured.

▲ This woman is clearing up outside a house destroyed in an air raid. Some "bombed-out" families went to live with relatives or neighbours. Others were given temporary shelter in Rest Centres and **billets**. Many soon moved back into patched-up homes.

September 1940

The Blitz on London begins. Many women become air raid wardens.

November 1940–May 1941

The bombing of British cities is at its worst. Ports such as Liverpool and industrial centres such as Coventry are badly hit.

June 1941

Clothes rationing begins in Britain. Women's Voluntary Service (WVS) volunteers staff clothing depots, to pass on used clothing to the homeless.

▲ In December 1941, US women firefighters worked hard after Japan's air attack on Pearl Harbor, Hawaii. The naval base and surrounding airfields were left ablaze, with burning ships, wrecked planes, and more than 2,000 people killed.

Terrors of mass bombing

Women in Germany and Japan suffered greatly from 1942 until 1945 as Allied aircraft bombed German and Japanese cities. In mass raids on the German cities of Cologne, Hamburg, and Dresden, thousands of women were killed or injured, and many more made homeless. In 1945 the Allies dropped the first atomic bombs, on the Japanese cities of Hiroshima and Nagasaki. Both cities were almost totally destroyed.

Eyewitness

Takeharu Terao was a student science-teacher assigned to war work in Hiroshima, Japan. Takeharu survived the atomic bomb attack on 6 August 1945.

"I witnessed a yellowish-scarlet plume rising like a candle high in the sky surrounded by pitch black swirling smoke. At the same moment … houses lifted a little and then crashed down to the ground, like dominoes. It was just like a white wave coming towards me while standing on the beach."

9

19 February 1942	May 1942	February 1945
Japanese planes bomb Darwin, the first air raid on an Australian city. Over 240 are killed.	Over 1,000 British bombers hit the German city of Cologne, which suffers over 250 raids during the war.	The German city of Dresden is devastated by a "fire-storm" started by Allied bombing. In March 1945, Tokyo in Japan suffers similar havoc.

Air raid defences

Governments tried to be prepared for air attacks. This was called "civil defence". Air raid sirens warned people of approaching bombers. Families were instructed how to use air raid shelters and gas masks (in case poison gas bombs were dropped). Women and men were trained to fight fires, rescue victims from bombed buildings, and give first aid to the injured.

Air raids in Britain

During the Blitz on Britain, in 1940–1941, Air Raid Precautions (ARP) wardens checked each neighbourhood to make sure no houses were showing lights in the blackout. After each raid, they reported bomb damage and any unexploded bombs. Women volunteers drove ambulances. Rest centres and canteens were run by the Women's Voluntary Service (WVS), who served drinks, sandwiches, and soup to victims and rescuers.

▲ Many US cities also used underground railway stations as air raid shelters. These people are taking cover in a subway station in New York.

In an air raid, many people crowded into public shelters, big enough for hundreds of families. In London, thousands of people spent nights in Underground railway stations. Many families had small Anderson air raid shelters in their gardens and back yards. Indoor shelters like metal cages were used as tables during the day, and slept in at night.

▶ Women of the Auxiliary Territorial Service (ATS) during the Blitz on Britain. Women crewed **searchlight batteries**, flew **barrage balloons**, and directed **anti-aircraft guns** and fighter pilots to shoot down bombers.

DANGER FROM THE AIR

Eyewitness

Elsie Lee, who lived in Walsall, England, in 1939, remembered:

"The first time we heard the air raid sirens I was in bed with my three children. Talk about panic stations. There was I jumping out of bed and shaking my fist at the sky, and calling Hitler all kinds of names."

▲ Air raids meant anxious nights in shelters. Women made drinks and sandwiches, tried to get children to sleep or read stories to calm them while bombs exploded above their heads.

In the News

"We want at least a million men and women, and we want them for work that in an emergency [war] would be exacting [difficult] and dangerous. The job is not an amusement in peace-time nor would it be a soft job in time of war."

This quotation is from a British government leaflet of 1938, calling for volunteers to become ARP helpers. By 1942, Britain had almost 20,000 full-time Civil Defence women workers, with more than 127,000 women helping part-time.

LOOKOUT IN THE BLACKOUT

UNTIL YOUR EYES GET USED TO THE DARKNESS
TAKE IT EASY

▶ Government posters warned civilians of the dangers. In Britain and in Germany, despite the bombing, most people "carried on" and public services were quickly restored.

WAR WORK

Allied governments needed women to work alongside men making weapons. In December 1941, all British women aged around 20 to 30 had to register for war work. US factories were also soon employing thousands of women.

Films, newspapers, and magazines showed women factory workers in trousers and headscarves, smiling as they made tanks and planes. British workers were heard cheerfully singing along to radio programmes such as *Music While You Work*. In real life, women found factory life exhausting. Many worked 10-hour **shifts** for five or six days a week. After work, they had children to care for, and a home to keep going. Girls who had never been away from home were sent to work, often to a town they did not know.

Different pay

Almost all women workers grumbled that they were paid less than men doing the same job. In 1943, women making aircraft engines at the Rolls-Royce factory in Glasgow, Scotland, went on strike. Some people thought this was very **unpatriotic**. When strikers marched through the city, they were jeered, until the crowds learned how unfairly such women were paid. Although they did get a pay rise, a skilled woman was still paid less than a skilled man.

▲ Factories hummed busily day and night to produce planes, guns, uniforms, and other war materials. Women learned new skills. Some worked alongside men, but others replaced men who had gone to join the armed forces.

1939

The German government awards "Mothers Cross" medals to women who have big families. Hitler thinks women should be mothers, not factory workers.

May 1940

The British government increases the working week in aircraft factories to 70 hours for each worker.

March 1941

More day and night nurseries are provided to help British working women with children.

Women at work

- By 1943, 90 per cent of single women and 80 per cent of married women in Britain were doing war work or in the armed services.

- Around 12 million American women were working in 1940 (in peacetime). By 1944, the number at work had risen to over 18 million.

- **Nazi** Germany did not call up women for factory work until 1943. Hitler thought that German women should raise children at home, not do "men's work".

- However, the Nazis did force women captives from occupied countries to work in their factories.

▲ Women firefighters like these risked being killed or wounded by damaged buildings falling on them, or unexploded bombs blowing up without any warning.

Joining the war effort

Between 1940 and 1944, the number of working women in the United States increased by over 50 per cent. Typical was Almira Bondelid of San Diego, who left her shop job to work for Convair (an aircraft manufacturer), and helped build B-24 Liberator bombers. Women wanted to help the war effort. Marie Owens worked at the Huntsville Arsenal, in Alabama, making **munitions**. Her husband was in the US Army. She told a reporter: "I am interested in carrying on here while the boys do the fighting over there ... The harder I work for them here, the sooner they will come home." This attitude was common among women in all countries at war.

13

December 1941
Women in Britain aged around 20 to 30 have to register for war work. By 1942, 8.5 million women aged 19–46 have been registered.

1942
The head of the US War Manpower Commission states that "no women responsible for the care of young children" should be made to work.

February 1943
Germany calls up all men and women aged 16–65 for war work. By 1944, women make up a third of Britain's engineering workforce.

Women build aircraft

Aircraft were a vital part of the war effort. Women helped to build them. In 1942, US President Franklin D. Roosevelt called on American factories to build 60,000 aircraft a year. Few people believed it was possible. But in 1943, US factories built almost 86,000 planes. The next year they built over 96,000.

Many factories had given up making peacetime goods. Instead, workers previously trained in making furniture or vacuum cleaners now had to assemble aircraft or radars, for example. Workers quickly learned new skills. And work went on in spite of air raids.

In the News

At first, the British government found it hard to get women to work in factories. Magazine articles tried to persuade people to do so. In December 1941 the *Woman's Own* magazine declared: "Many women and girls still hesitate to volunteer for factory work because it's 'not quite nice'. Don't they know that some of the finest women in Britain are in industry now? Do they think the Nazis are quite nice!"

▲ Women handled heavy machinery as well as assembling small parts for precision equipment. This woman is boring a cylinder block, part of an engine for a propeller-driven fighter or bomber plane. Posters in factories urged workers to do their job faster and build more planes.

Eyewitness

Muriel Simkin worked in a munitions (weapons) factory in Dagenham, Essex, England. She remembered air raids.

"On one occasion a bomb hit the factory before we were given permission to go to the shelter. The paint department went up. I saw several people flying through the air and I just ran home ... It was a terrible job but we had no option ... We were risking our lives in the same way as the soldiers were."
Interviewed in *Voices from the Past: The Blitz* (1987)

We Can Do It!

WAR PRODUCTION CO-ORDINATING COMMITTEE

▲ Millions of American women worked in aircraft factories. They earned the nickname "Rosie the Riveter". Rosie was a character in a government advertising campaign.

▲ Sewing silk for parachutes. A mistake in packing the parachute and its long cords could cost the life of an airman leaping from a burning plane.

▼ This graph shows how the USA boosted its aircraft production after it entered the war in 1941. It was soon building more planes than any other country.

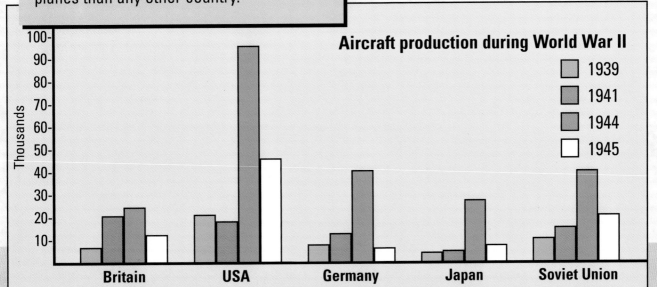

Aircraft production during World War II

1939
1941
1944
1945

Thousands

Britain   USA   Germany   Japan   Soviet Union

FEEDING THE FAMILY

Food was as vital to the war effort as guns and planes. Britain imported much of its food in ships from the United States, Canada, and Australia. But hundreds of ships were sunk by German submarines.

Farmers were urged to grow more food, while people got used to "going without". Starvation was worst in China and in the Soviet Union (where many farmers were driven from the land by the German invasion in 1941). But hunger was common in occupied countries – where the Nazis kept the best food for themselves. By 1945, many Japanese were surviving on one meal a day of rice mixed with soya beans, or dumplings made from ground wheat and grass. In many countries, women had to feed families as best they could, and on farms, women took over jobs previously done by men.

Rationing for all

In Britain, food rationing began in 1940, starting with bacon, sugar, meat, tea, and butter. Everyone was issued with a ration book and shopkeepers could only sell food in exchange for coupons from the book. The United States brought in some rationing in 1942, as did Australia.

▶ Shoppers in the United States wait in a queue to buy rations of sugar – a familiar wartime experience.

16

November 1940

A WVS food convoy of eight trucks with 27 women volunteers delivers emergency food from London to the bombed city of Coventry. Food convoys continue until 1944.

May 1941

The first US ship with special war food supplies reaches Britain.

June 1941

Clothes are rationed in Britain. People need 16 coupons for a raincoat, or 7 coupons for a pair of shoes.

▶ The United States shipped tonnes of food to Britain and the Soviet Union during the war. Cargoes of square-sided cans of Spam, canned meat first sold in the United States in 1937, arrived along with powdered eggs, Hershey chocolate bars, chewing gum, and other unfamiliar delights.

Leaner and fitter – but some odd dishes

In spite of shortages, most people kept fit. Few people became overweight, and rationing did guarantee fair shares of basic foods for all. Cooks were urged to try familiar foods in unfamiliar ways (meat pies without meat, for example). Sugar was rationed, so many people gave up sugar in tea and coffee. Jam and chocolate were treats. There were many suggestions for unusual "wild" foods, such as cormorants' eggs, seaweed, rosehip marmalade, and roast squirrel. In Germany, women made coffee from ground acorns, after supplies of imported coffee beans dried up.

Eyewitness

In the United States, Mary Gardner of Rhode Island (whose father went fishing) remembered her wartime diet, "we ate a lot of fish because meat was rationed ... you had to buy things that were going to stretch [make a lot of meals], maybe spaghetti, macaroni ... and mix it up with something else."

Quoted in *An Oral History of Rhode Island Women, South Kingstown High School*

17

1942

The Office of Price Administration set up a rationing scheme in the United States. Coffee is one of the items rationed.

July 1942

Sweets are rationed in Britain. Also in 1942, Australia launches its own "save-it" campaign, with some rationing.

February 1943

US shoppers are rationed to three pairs of new shoes a year. In Britain, the ration is one pair.

Vegetables for victory

Women were urged to "dig for victory". This meant growing vegetables in gardens, backyards, public parks – anywhere there was a patch of soil. Schools joined in, with children and teachers planting beans, tomatoes, potatoes, cabbages, and peas in what Americans called "Victory gardens".

Working on the land

To replace men farmworkers, young British women joined the Women's Land Army. The experience could be a nasty shock. British teenager Betty Attwood (age 17) was sent to cut timber. She lodged with a country family, shivering in bed beneath "two torn sheets, threadbare blankets, and thin quilts". She and her friend piled coats and rugs on the bed, but were still cold when they scrambled out before dawn for breakfast – "one slice of bread and margarine, and a cup of tea".

For a healthy, happy job

Join the WOMEN'S LAND ARMY

for details:
APPLY TO NEAREST W.L.A. COUNTY OFFICE OR TO W.L.A. HEADQUARTERS 6 CHESHAM PLACE LONDON S.W.1
Issued by the Ministry of Agriculture and the Ministry of Labour and National Service

▼ This American boy is being handed his first ration book. To make up for the shortage of protein foods, such as meat, fish, and eggs (all rationed), mothers were encouraged to serve more vegetables.

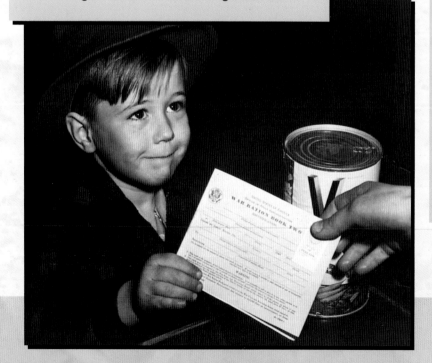

▲ Formed during World War I, the Land Army was re-formed in 1939. By 1945, Britain had around 80,000 "land girls". Posters like this showed happy workers enjoying harvest-time. Most young women, often from big cities, found farm work cold and wet, bruising, and back-aching. But they stuck at it.

◀ A land girl ploughing. The farm day was long and the work tough. In the 1940s, many farmers still used horses, not tractors, and even machine-threshing (separating wheat grain from the ears) needed up to twelve workers. Some men workers made "new girls" do the dirtiest jobs.

Eyewitness

"We looked like monks from the Middle Ages, standing there with sacks around our middles, another sack over our heads ..."

This was how one Land Army girl recalled picking sprouts in winter. Others found that one of their jobs was rat-catching. Rats were called "Hitler's little chums" because they ate grain stores, so as many rats as possible were killed.

GARDEN
V
IN 1945
VICTORY

GROW YOUR OWN *Be sure!*

19

▶ Americans also needed to grow and preserve fruit and vegetables. A wartime slogan in the USA was "Grow your own. Be sure!" The message behind this was that home-grown vegetables were healthy, as well as helping the war effort. "Growing your own" was good for everyone.

WOMEN UNDER FIRE

Women served in the army, navy, and air force, though few fought in combat. Some flew fighter and bomber planes. Others carried out dangerous missions behind enemy lines.

In 1939, Britain had 43,000 women in the services. By 1942 there were 400,000. Women did many jobs. They were cooks, clerks, drivers, electricians, code experts, radio operators, pilots, parachute packers, and meteorologists (weather experts). A few became secret agents in occupied countries helping the **Resistance**. Only in the Soviet Union did women fight alongside, and against, men. More than half the 800,000 women in the Soviet Army served as machine-gunners, tank drivers, **snipers**, combat pilots, and first-aiders.

Women pilots

American and Commonwealth women were not allowed to fly in combat, but they ferried new aircraft from factories to air force bases. Two famous wartime pilots were 1930s air racer Jacqueline Cochran, who led the US Women's Flying Training Detachment (WFTD) and Britain's Amy Johnson. In 1930 Johnson had flown solo from Britain to Australia, and during the war she piloted warplanes with Britain's Air Transport Auxiliary (ATA).

▶ Jacqueline Cochran (shown here after the war) won fame in the 1930s as a pilot in air races. During World War II she led the US women pilots, or WASPs. After the war, she flew jets and became the fastest woman pilot in the world.

March 1941
Women join the new Women's Auxiliary Australian Air Force. About 27,000 have enlisted by 1945.

April 1941
British women's services become officially part of the armed services, under the same military rules as men.

1941
Amy Johnson, flying a military plane, is killed when it crashes into the sea.

▶ A woman pilot with an RAF plane. Women flew new planes from factories to air bases. They also helped flight-test equipment, such as radios.

Better at home?

The Nazis thought women should stay at home, having babies, not wear army uniform. Some Nazis even disapproved of women wearing trousers! But this did not stop German women doing war work as civilians. For example, pilot Hanna Reisch tested new, experimental warplanes. She courageously flew messages in and out of Berlin during the last terrible days of battle in that city before Hitler's death in 1945.

In the News

In 1942, a US War Department booklet told American soldiers coming to Britain, "British women have proved themselves in this war ... When you see a girl in uniform with a bit of ribbon on her tunic, remember she didn't get it for knitting more socks than anyone else..."

Women at work

USA

- Women's Army Corps (WAC). By 1944, there were around 100,000 WACs.
- Women's Reserve of the United States Naval Reserve

Britain

- Women's Royal Naval Service (WRNS or Wrens)
- Women's Auxiliary Air Force (WAAFs)
- Auxiliary Territorial Service (ATS)

May 1942
The Women's Army Auxiliary Corps (WAAC) is formed in the United States.

1943
The US Women's Flying Training Detachment (WFTD) merges with the Women's Auxiliary Ferrying Squadron to form the WASPs (Women Airforce Service Pilots).

June 1944
Army nurses are among the first women in uniform to serve in Normandy, France, soon after the D-Day landings.

Captured by the enemy

Working as a secret agent was one of the most dangerous jobs in wartime. There were no rules. A soldier in uniform, if captured, must be treated properly as a prisoner of war. A captured agent, with no uniform, could be shot as a spy. Defying the risks, brave women volunteered to parachute into occupied countries to help the resistance to the Nazis. Among them were Nancy Wake, Odette Sansom, and Noor-un-Nisa Inayat Khan.

Women captives

Many women civilians were imprisoned or forced to work in labour camps by the Nazis and Japanese. In Europe, millions of Jewish women and children were herded into **concentration camps** and put to death by the Nazis during the Holocaust.

In the News

"Few if any women have been decorated so highly for their exploits during the Second World War." The media praised Nancy Wake (then aged 91), who in 2004 was made a Companion of the Order of Australia. Honoured for her wartime courage, she said modestly, "I hope I am worth it."

▲ Nancy Wake was born in New Zealand and raised in Australia. In 1939, she was living in France. She escaped to Britain, but parachuted back into occupied France as a secret agent. In France, she carried messages by bicycle and **sabotaged** factories. The Germans nicknamed her the "White Mouse", because she was so hard to catch.

WOMEN UNDER FIRE

◀ Agent Odette Sansom (a French woman married to an Englishman) had the code name "Lise". In 1943 she was captured by the Germans, but this is what she thought of her captors: "They will kill me physically, but that's all. They won't win anything." She survived almost two years in a concentration camp, was honoured after the war for her bravery, and died in 1995.

Profile of a secret agent

- Noor-un-Nisa Inayat Khan had American and Indian parents. Raised in France, she knew the language and the people.

- Trained as an agent in England, she was given the code name "Madeleine". She travelled with a radio hidden in a suitcase. Her job was to pass messages between England and the French Resistance.

- She was captured in 1943 by the **Gestapo**, tortured, and shot.

◀ Women agents carried with them a small radio like this one, which could be hidden in a suitcase. Radio operators moved frequently, from house to house, because the Gestapo could trace messages radioed from the same place night after night.

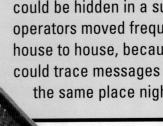

KEEP SMILING

Even in war, people still had some leisure time. Entertainment, and news, came from radio, films, newspapers, and magazines. Women did their best to keep up spirits, as entertainers and as family members.

Radio times

Television in Britain had begun in the 1930s, but not many people had it, so radio ruled the airwaves. People listened to radio news reports, and to broadcasts by war leaders. US President Roosevelt gave "Fireside Chats", while British Prime Minister Winston Churchill made stirring speeches. Both sides used **propaganda**, but the radio broadcasts by "Lord Haw Haw" (speaking from Germany) and "Tokyo Rose" (from Japan), full of boasts and threats, caused more amusement than alarm. Many women listened to serious talk programmes about current events and what would happen after the war.

Popular music and film

- Many women were fans of male "crooners" [singers] such as Americans Bing Crosby and Frank Sinatra.

- There were many women singers too, such as Adelaide Hall, Judy Garland, the Andrews Sisters, Vera Lynn, and Anne Shelton.

- An all-woman dance band was led by Ivy Benson.

- Popular wartime films included *Gone With the Wind*, *The Wizard of Oz*, *Mrs Miniver* (an American view of a British family at war), and Shakespeare's *Henry V*.

▲ Dancehalls were packed most weekends. Muriel Castledine, a nurse in the British naval town of Devonport, liked the "Paul Jones" dance, when "boys formed the outside ring and girls the inner one, and we walked round... and stopped opposite a new partner when the band broke off... It was magic."

September 1939
ENSA, the armed forces entertainment organization, is set up in Britain. It sends shows all over the world to entertain troops.

July 1941
The "V for Victory" signal, "da-da-da-dah" (from Beethoven's 5th symphony), is first used by the BBC to introduce news bulletins to occupied Europe.

October 1942
Shops start selling cardboard wedding cakes, after the British government bans icing-sugar cake toppings.

◀ At Christmas people celebrated as best they could, remembered loved ones far away, and hoped that next year the war would be over for good.

▼ Singer Adelaide Hall was one popular wartime entertainer.

Entertainment for all

Music and laughter did most to keep up people's spirits. Popular comedians included Elsie and Doris Waters in Britain, and Gracie Allen in the United States. Women entertainers such as film star Betty Grable and singer Vera Lynn toured the war zones. In deserts and jungles, singers, dancers, and actors emerged from tents or army trucks to perform, even when bombs or shells started to fall nearby. People hummed the latest hit tunes while they worked, and went to the cinema to forget the war for a couple of hours.

Parties to celebrate

Women kept up family morale. They wrote letters to faraway husbands, sons, or brothers, and they produced food, drink, and presents for birthdays, Christmas, Thanksgiving, and home-coming parties. The best parties broke out in streets and homes in 1945. On VE Day (8 May) and VJ Day (14 August), people celebrated the end of the war, first in Europe and then in the Pacific.

Eyewitness

Jean Pountney went into town (at Melton Mowbray, Leicestershire, England) for dances on Wednesday nights and met her first GIs.

"The Americans had all the latest records. I'd seen jiving before, but not the way they did it. I was dancing with one chap and suddenly he swept me off my feet!"

25

1942	September 1944	December 1944
To help newly arriving US troops in Britain feel at home, American Red Cross girls serve coffee and doughnuts from trucks.	After five years, the blackout is lifted in Britain. Women no longer carry torches when out at night.	American bandleader Glenn Miller, a favourite radio broadcaster, is presumed killed when his plane disappears on a flight from England to France.

Love and marriage

In the war many people made lasting friendships, and lifelong partnerships. Men and women were often thrown together by chance meetings – working together, waiting for a bus or train, or getting lost in the blackout. Many married couples were separated during the war and lots of children grew up without fathers around. More marriages broke up – in Britain, the divorce rate increased from 1 in 100 in 1939 to 5 in 100 by the end of the war.

KEEP SMILING

▶ Homecoming, in 1945. Some separated couples managed to meet at occasional weekends, but for others, years passed before they were reunited. Letters were the only way to keep in touch.

GI brides

- From 1942, thousands of American troops, nicknamed "GIs", arrived in Britain.

- About 80,000 British women married American servicemen. Most then went to live in the United States. Newspapers called them "GI brides".

▶ Couples who decided to marry during the war often had to arrange a quick "no frills" wedding before the bride or groom went back to the military or war work. Popular songs such as *We'll Meet Again* and *I'll Be Seeing You* captured the mood of the times.

A threat to family life?

Many women ran a home, worked long hours, and did volunteer activities, such as selling war bonds (to raise money), collecting unwanted clothing, and tending vegetable plots. Not everyone thought this was admirable.

Critics said women at work let their children run wild. And many women said they disapproved of the "new habit" of women going to bars and pubs on their own.

▶ Couples separated by the war often shared favourite songs. Hit tunes were sold on records and in songbooks, like these.

THE IMPACT OF WAR

World War II had an enormous impact on society. For women who lost families and friends, life would never be the same. They were left with sad memories. But not all memories were painful. Many women had fun, made new friends, travelled the world, and learned new skills.

Many men who worked alongside women appreciated their abilities and courage. Even so, when peace came in 1945, women still faced an uphill struggle for equal pay at work and fair treatment.

The war's legacy

Today, women fly fighter planes and command warships. Women hold top jobs in government and industry. World War II helped bring about the "women's rights" movement because millions of women at war had gained in confidence and ambition. In 1940, the editor of *Aeroplane* magazine had written: "… there are millions of women who could do useful jobs in war. But the trouble is … so many insist on wanting to do jobs which they are quite incapable of doing."

By 1945, most people knew that women were capable of doing almost anything.

Eyewitnesses

"This war more than any other war in history is a woman's war."

John G. Winant, US ambassador to Britain during the war.

"The girls lived like men, fought like men and, alas, some of them died like men. Unarmed, they showed great courage."

Lt General Sir Frederick Pile, commander of British anti-aircraft defences

▲ VE Day, Tuesday 8 May 1945, marked the end of the war in Europe. By August, with the defeat of Japan, the war was finally over. "I wonder if the world has learned the lesson of war this time," Muriel Green, a shopworker in Somerset, England, wrote in her diary.
Quote from *Mass Observation – Wartime Women*

TIMELINE

1939

1 September Germany invades Poland.
3 September Britain and France declare war on Germany. Thousands of British troops leave for France. Many mothers have already parted with children, evacuated to the countryside.

1940

January Butter, bacon, and eggs are rationed in Britain.
April Germany invades Denmark and Norway.
May Germany invades Belgium, the Netherlands, and France. Many women become refugees. Women join the Resistance.
June Italy joins Germany in the Axis alliance. France surrenders.
July The German air force begins attacks on Britain. Women help in the defence.
September The Blitz begins. Women serve as ARP wardens.

1941

March Australia recruits more women to its armed forces.
April Germany invades Greece and Yugoslavia. The British women's services are made part of the armed forces.
May The United States begins shipping food rations to Britain.
June Germany invades the Soviet Union. Soviet women fight alongside men in the army. Clothes rationing begins in Britain.
7 December The Japanese attack on Pearl Harbor brings the United States into the war.
December British women aged around 20 to 30 must register for war work. Work registration soon includes women aged 19 to 46.

1942

January–February Singapore and the Philippines fall to the Japanese, who threaten Australia.
May The US Army women's branch, the WAAC, is set up.
8 June Two Japanese submarines shell the Australian cities of Sydney and Newcastle.
August US troops land in the Solomon Islands, at Guadalcanal
September The Germans and Russians fight for Stalingrad, in the Soviet Union.
October–November The Allies win the Battle of El Alamein in North Africa.
November American shoppers find that coffee is rationed. The US government calls for more women to join the armed forces.
December American troops in Britain celebrate Christmas. Many British women meet Americans for the first time.

1943

February The Allied bombing of Germany increases. German women are called up for war work.
February A German army surrenders at Stalingrad.
May The Allies drive the Axis forces out of North Africa.
July The Allies land in Sicily, Italy. The Allies also begin the recapture of islands from the Japanese in the Pacific.
December One third of Britain's engineering workers are women.

1944

Women in weapons factories earn £10 a week – three times the average woman's wage in 1939.
June Women in Britain experience frightening new air attacks by V-1 flying bombs.
6 June D-Day; Allied armies land in France to begin the liberation of Western Europe. Women nurses follow the invasion troops.
25 August France's capital city, Paris, is liberated.
September The blackout in Britain is eased. The first V-2 rocket hits London.
October The Allies begin the recapture of the Philippines.

1945

January Many German families are near starvation.
February Fierce fighting after US forces land on Iwo Jima, close to Japan's main islands. Many Japanese kill themselves rather than surrender.
14 February The German city of Dresden is destroyed by bombing raids.
April Survivors are rescued from Nazi concentration camps, where millions of people have been put to death.
30 April Hitler kills himself in Berlin as Soviet armies capture the German capital city.
7 May Germany surrenders. Millions of women are among the refugees.
6 August Allies drop an atomic bomb on the Japanese city of Hiroshima, and another on Nagasaki three days later. Japan surrenders.
14 August Crowds celebrate V-J (Victory over Japan) Day. The war is over. Families are reunited and people begin rebuilding their lives.

GLOSSARY

Allied nations Britain, France, Canada, Australia, the Soviet Union, the United States, Poland, and other countries that fought together against Germany, Italy, and Japan

anti-aircraft guns big guns firing shells thousands of metres into the air to hit or scare off enemy planes

barrage balloons large balloons on wire cables, used as a defence against low-flying aircraft

battery group of guns or searchlights

billet temporary home, usually where people share another family's house

blackout measures to reduce all lights at night, to hide possible targets from enemy bombers

Blitz the German bombing attack on London and other British cities

civil defence arrangements to protect towns and cities from enemy attack, especially from the air

concentration camp prison camp in which captives are kept without proper housing, food, or medical treatment

Gestapo German secret police hunting Allied agents and Resistance fighters

GIs nickname for American soldiers; short for General Issue (referring to standard clothes given to all soldiers)

morale spirit of the people in a country at war

munitions ammunition, explosives, guns, and other combat material

Nazi member of the National Socialist German Workers' Party, led by Adolf Hitler

occupied country a country that is conquered and then ruled by an invader

propaganda control of information in the media so as to show your own side in a good light and the enemy in a bad way

rationing government control of the sale of food, fuel, clothes, and other goods

refugee homeless person fleeing in search of safety during wartime

Resistance members of an organization fighting enemy forces that have occupied their country

sabotage to break equipment, slow down work in a factory, or in other ways harm an enemy's war effort

searchlight large electric lamp used to pick out enemy planes in the night sky, as targets for guns

shift period of work in a factory, usually about 8 hours but often longer in wartime

siren device that makes a loud wailing noise, as a warning

sniper sharpshooter trained to shoot at enemy soldiers, usually from a concealed position

telegram urgent communication sent by phone line, but delivered to an address as a short printed message

unpatriotic someone thought to be acting against the best interests of the country

widow a married woman whose husband has died

FINDING OUT MORE

If you are interested in finding out more about World War II, here are some more books and websites you might find useful.

Further reading

Your local public library's adult section should have plenty of war books, including books about what it was like to be a woman during World War II. Written by people who were actually there, such books will give you an idea of what ordinary women thought about the war and their part in it.

Books for younger readers

Causes of World War II, Paul Dowswell (Heinemann Library, 2002)

History Through Poetry; World War II, Reg Grant (Hodder Wayland, 2001)

The Day the War was Won, Colin Hymion (Ticktock Media, 2003)

WW2 Stories: War at Home, Anthony Masters (Franklin Watts, 2004)

WW2 True Stories, Clive Gifford (Hodder Children's Books, 2002)

Books for older readers

Combat Nurse, Eric Taylor (Robert Hale, 1999)

Wartime Women – A Mass Observation anthology, edited by Dorothy Sheridan (Heinemann, 1990)

Women at War: In Uniform, Carol Harris (Sutton, 2003)

Women at War: The Home Front, Carol Harris (Sutton, 2000)

Websites

http://www.womenofcourage.com – this website looks at the courage of US women pilots during World War II.

http://www.wartimememories.co.uk/ – a website containing wartime recollections, including those of women who lived through World War II.

http://bbc.co.uk/history/war/wwtwo/ – this website from the BBC has lots of resources about World War II.

INDEX